WALKING *in* PURPOSE

HEALING FROM THE INSIDE OUT

DOMINIQUE WHITNEY

Walking in Purpose

Copyright © 2025 Dominque Whitney. All rights reserved. Published and designed by Ministry Event Marketing. Printed in the United States of America

ISBN: 979-8-9986757-6-8 Paperback

Disclaimer This publication is designed to provide accurate and authoritative information regarding the subject matter covered. No part of this book may be reproduced, stored in a retrieval system, or transmitted in any form or by any means, electronic, mechanical, photocopying, recording, or otherwise, without express written permission of the author or publisher, except by a reviewer who may quote brief passages in a review.

Unauthorized distribution, sale, or resale of any such property will result in legal action to compensate the trust for the unauthorized use of its private property.

Scriptures marked NIV are taken from the NEW INTERNATIONAL VERSION (NIV): Scripture taken from THE HOLY BIBLE, NEW INTERNATIONAL VERSION ®. Copyright© 1973, 1978, 1984, 2011 by Biblica, Inc.™. Used by permission of Zondervan.

Scripture taken from the New King James Version®. Copyright © 1982 by Thomas Nelson. Used by permission. All rights reserved.

Scriptures marked KJV are taken from the KING JAMES VERSION (KJV): KING JAMES VERSION, public domain.

Walking in Purpose

Table of Contents

Acknowledgement...7
Chapter One:..9
   The Beginning of Rejection
Chapter Two:..13
   The Thoughts of God
Chapter Three:...17
   The Diagnosis
Chapter Four:...21
   The Principle of Healing
Chapter Five:..27
   The Boundaries
Chapter Six:..33
   Deliverance
Chapter Seven:...37
   Forgiveness
Chapter Eight:..41
   Declarations

Walking in Purpose

Acknowledgement

"To my husband, Steve Whitney, whose patience and understanding saw me through the writing process." Thank you to my mom and dad for raising me up in the way that I wouldn't depart from Christ. I am deeply grateful to my brothers, Alex and Randy Collins, who have been my protectors both growing up and now. Thank you for all that you are doing for me. I love you both with my whole heart.

Thank you to Supt. N. Carter, Mother F. Carter, Mother B. Matthews, and the late Elder E. Matthews Sr. for your guidance and being an example of Christ. Training me to be the woman of God I am today.

Thank you to my Apostle Vincent Campbell for helping me to birth this book. Thank you for taking me through

Walking in Purpose

Deliverance and for unlocking everything that was locked up inside me and pushing me to my destiny.

Thank you, Pastor (Momma) Frances Campbell, for taking me and my husband in as family. Thank you for also walking me through deliverance and getting me all together when I need it. Your family holds a special place in my heart.

Thank you to this special, beautiful prophetess, Nicole Phillip. Thank you for believing in me and encouraging me not to quit but to keep pushing because there is more. I thank God for you; it's an honor to know you.

Chapter One:
The Beginning of Rejection

As a child, you're supposed to be happy and love the life you're living. However, for some children, this is not the case. A child would never imagine that their world would collapse, transitioning from a carefree dream world to a terrifying reality. The verbal and mental abuse starts with statements like, "You will never amount to anything." I don't understand why I'm wasting my time with you. You act just like the other parent. Every time I look at your face, you remind me of the other parent. I'm going to go with the others and leave you here."

The child doesn't know what to do but retreat to their room, listening to music to keep from breaking down and crying. One important thing the child starts doing is praying, asking God to help them get through these challenging times. Some parents bury themselves in work to avoid dealing with the life and issues happening around them, which also means they are being abused in some way. The children see the situation and know how they are supposed to be treated.

The child begins to go over to a friend's house, feeling safe there. The child, however, is silently crying out for help. A few of the child's friends show signs of experiencing various forms of abuse at home. Eventually, things fade away, but the child remains so broken that it starts affecting their schoolwork. The child no longer wants to be at home and instead buries themselves in music to cope. They get involved in extracurricular activities at school just to stay occupied.

Walking in Purpose

How many people can cope with having dysfunctional family issues? Many people cope with their struggles by using alcohol, drugs, lashing out, and other forms of escape. Depression sets in, followed by low self-esteem and low confidence. Some individuals may begin experiencing suicidal thoughts. We've lost so many people to suicide. Here in Tampa, FL, the suicide rate is high, especially at the airport and the Skyway Bridge.

Chapter Two:
The Thoughts of God

I remember my mom would often have to call the pastor to come and pray over me because the enemy would try to attack me. After he finished praying, he would give me instructions to follow and then go home. I would notice that these attacks often happened at night. My mom told me that as a baby, all I would do at night was cry, and I wouldn't stop until the pastor came and prayed. She said that after he prayed, I stopped crying. God gave me peace to rest.

In 1984, at the age of 8, our church had a week-long revival. After the service on the final night, I approached Pastor N. Carter and expressed my desire for salvation. He called over Pastor E. Matthews, and together they brought me to Christ. That night, I gave my life to Christ, and it was the best day of my life. These leaders checked on me and encouraged me throughout the process. A few months later, I was at a Sunday evening service. I remember going up to the front row, kneeling down, and my aunt, the mothers, and the deacons surrounded me. They began to tarry with me, and I received the Holy Ghost. It was just like fire. I spoke in unknown tongues, and I began to rejoice and praise God in a dance.

Growing up, I loved to sing, speak, and encourage others, but I would get shut down. I began to dislike my voice and the way I sounded. When I wasn't able to use my voice in the ways I wanted, I completely shut down. People would ask me to sing, but I would say, "Nope." The only time I would open up to sing was at school, around my peers, because I didn't feel judged. They encouraged me to sing,

Walking in Purpose

and we had a wonderful time. However, in church, I didn't sing as freely as I did in school. I knew God was going to use my voice. I was so frustrated and started to question God as the tears begin to roll down my face God, my heart is your house. Why am I being shut down to where I can't speak what you wanted me to say and to worship and praise you like I'm supposed to? I made my room in my house where I can freely pray, worship, and praise God. I stayed lying prostrate before God.

Family members began molesting me at an early age. This opened up the door for the spirit of perversion, lust, pornography, alcohol, and smoking weed in my life. I used these substances as a coping mechanism to deal with the challenges in my life. Question what I did to deserve to be treated this way, and I know that touching little children like that wasn't normal.

Walking in Purpose

Two people raped me on the same day, one after the other, and it really broke me down. I was already an alcoholic; it drove me to drink even more in an attempt to numb the pain of that traumatic experience. I told a few people and kept it a secret for years because in my mind I was saying, Why me? This allowed more spirits to enter, and the spirits in them transferred to me. I would be praying, asking God to heal the wound, because it was still there after sobering up. What killed others; it didn't kill me.

My insecurities about my looks, my body, my stomach, my facial hair, and how my clothes looked on me because of my shape made me let it get in the way of life. Trying to please others instead of being who God told me who I am. Being me and loving me.

Chapter Three:
The Diagnosis

At fifteen, I was diagnosed with PCOS (Polycystic Ovary Syndrome). I had cysts on my ovaries. The experience was horrible at that age. Sometimes, I would go without my menstrual cycle for months at a time, and then it would reverse, and I felt like the woman with the issue of blood. I had to trust God that one day He would heal me from this issue of blood that lasted for 18 years. The process was no joke. I had to push my way through it. I was always weak and in severe pain, but I kept singing and praising God, trusting that He would come through. I kept pushing.

Around 2008-2009, I was told that there was a mass in my ovaries and that I had cancer. I began to cry and started praying. I didn't want my parents to know, so I told my middle brother. What did he do? He spilled the news to my mom. In 2011-2012, I had the doctor run some tests to see what was happening with my PCOS. She scheduled an appointment for a sonogram. The very next day, the doctor personally called me. "Ms. Collins, I just called to let you know I got your results back," she said. "Ms. Collins, the cysts on your ovaries are gone."

In 2018, I had some tests done again here in Florida. When the results came back, the doctor said the reason for the follow-up tests was because my last test had shown abnormal results. She continued, "I just want to let you know that everything is fine. In the sonogram, we found no cysts. All I see is a lot of eggs that were produced."

At the age of 17, I was diagnosed with asthma, and I had to carry a breathing pump. In 2009, I woke up on a Sunday

Walking in Purpose

morning, getting ready for the Church Anniversary Service, when I had an asthma attack. My family rushed me to the E.R., but the nurse didn't believe us. She kicked the doctor out of the room, and when she started examining me, she told us, "You're right; she's having an asthma attack." I had three rounds of breathing treatment, and the doctor came in and told my parents that they were giving me a nebulizer machine that I would have to carry everywhere I went.

Well, I'm here to report that I don't carry my machine anymore. When I tell you God is a healer, all you need to do is trust Him, and He'll do the rest. Trust the healing process.

In my 20s, I was diagnosed with diabetes. My A1C was between 500 and 600, and insulin was given.

Chapter Four:
The Principle of Healing

Listen, God is a healer. There may be someone reading this who is going through the same thing. Just hold on—God has not forgotten about you. He is going to heal you; just keep trusting and believing.

How was I healed from this issue? I started by forgiving the people who had done things to me. I stopped holding on to the grudges from my childhood. I let go of the anger that had been inside me, because it was killing me from the inside out. I had to go through a deliverance process to get everything out of me.

Healing also comes with repentance, striving to be pure in the eyes of Christ. When God heals us, we must gain

Walking in Purpose

wisdom on how to stay healed.

1. Watch What We Put in Our Temple: Our bodies are temples of the Holy Spirit, and what we feed ourselves; physically, emotionally, and spiritually—directly affects our health and healing. It's important to be mindful of the things we expose ourselves to, whether it's the food we eat, the media we consume, or the company we keep. Just as a healthy diet nurtures the body, wholesome and uplifting thoughts nurture the mind and spirit. Taking care of our temple is not just about what we eat, but also about creating an environment that promotes healing, peace, and positivity. Let go of the things that bring toxicity into your life and make space for the things that bring health, vitality, and strength.

2. Pray and Fast: Prayer and fasting are powerful tools in the healing process. Prayer allows us to communicate with God, share our burdens, and seek His guidance and strength. It's in those quiet moments of prayer that we often hear God's voice most clearly, offering comfort and clarity. Fasting, on the other hand, is a way to humble ourselves before God and seek spiritual breakthrough. It helps us draw nearer to God, strengthens our resolve, and allows us to focus on His will instead of our own desires. Through prayer and fasting, we can experience deeper healing, spiritual renewal, and clarity for the path ahead.

3. Read the Word: The Word of God is life and healing. Scripture is filled with promises of peace, restoration, and healing. When we immerse ourselves in the Word, it renews our minds, heals our wounds, and strengthens our spirit. The Bible says in Proverbs 4:20-22, "My son, give attention to my words; incline your ear to my sayings. Do

Walking in Purpose

not let them depart from your eyes; keep them in the midst of your heart; for they are life to those who find them, and health to all their flesh." Reading the Word is not just about gaining knowledge—it's about internalizing God's truth and allowing it to work healing in every area of our lives.

4. Clean Eating and Drinking: Healing doesn't just take place in the spirit; it also involves the body. Clean eating and drinking is a way of honoring our bodies as temples of the Holy Spirit. Choose whole, nutritious foods that fuel your body, and avoid processed foods and substances that can drain your energy or contribute to illness. Hydration is just as important—drinking enough water is essential to keep the body functioning at its best. A healthy diet can improve mental clarity, restore physical strength, and create the right conditions for emotional and spiritual healing. Healing is a holistic process that requires a healthy mind, body, and spirit, so take care of all aspects of your well-being.

5. Stay Focused: One of the biggest challenges in maintaining healing is staying focused. It's easy to get distracted by circumstances, negative thoughts, or past wounds. But healing requires us to keep our eyes fixed on God, trusting in His timing and His power to restore. Stay focused on your healing journey, and refuse to be distracted by the things that may try to pull you back into unhealthy patterns. Set your heart and mind on the goal of wholeness, and take each step with purpose and intentionality. Focus on gratitude, faith, and the truth of God's promises. When we stay focused on the path of healing, we give ourselves the best chance for lasting transformation and peace.

I speak wholeness over your life. I speak healing over your

Walking in Purpose

broken heart, that God will fill the empty hole.

Chapter Five:
The Boundaries

We find that personal boundaries are violated every second through abusive relationships, such as verbal, mental, physical, and sexual abuse. These violations can lead to destructive behaviors, like alcoholism, as a way of coping with a lack of boundaries. What many don't realize is that turning to alcohol or putting others down won't solve the problems; you have to face them head-on. Emotional distance in families can also be a result of hurtful words, physical force, manipulation, and control.

Walking in Purpose

As 2 Timothy 3:1-5 warns:

1. Know also, that in the last days perilous times shall come.
2. For men shall be lovers of their own selves, covetous, boasters, proud, blasphemers, disobedient to parents, unthankful, and unholy.
3. Without natural affection, truce-breakers, false accusers, incontinent, fierce, despisers of those that are good.
4. Traitors, heady, high-minded, lovers of pleasures more than lovers of God;
5. Having a form of godliness but denying the power thereof: from such turn away.

In situations where boundaries are constantly violated, it's important to recognize that the hurt inflicted often stems from deep emotional wounds that need healing.

Walking in Purpose

Sometimes, we unintentionally repeat these patterns in our own lives, treating others the same way we were treated, not realizing that it's not the way things are supposed to be.

Galatians 4:17 says, "They zealously affect you, but not well; yea, they would exclude you, that ye might affect them." And Titus 3:5 reminds us that, "Not by works of righteousness which we have done, but according to His mercy He saved us, by the washing of regeneration, and renewing of the Holy Ghost."

A controlling spirit disrespects others' boundaries and rarely maintains healthy boundaries themselves. This behavior is often associated with witchcraft, as it seeks to manipulate and dominate others. Coping with such issues can sometimes lead us to develop similar controlling behaviors, which only perpetuate the cycle. However,

Walking in Purpose

when you realize that this is not the way things are meant to be, you can start the journey of healing and establishing healthy boundaries.

Here are steps to help you on your healing journey:

1. **Surrender your life to God.**
2. **Develop a prayer life.**
3. **Confess the lack of boundaries**—acknowledge that unhealthy patterns exist.
4. **Go through deliverance.**
5. **Immerse yourself in the Word of Healing.**

    Philippians 4:8 says, *"Finally, brethren, whatsoever things are true, whatsoever things are honest, whatsoever things are just, whatsoever things are pure, whatsoever things are lovely, whatsoever things are of good report; if there be any virtue, and if there be any praise, think on these things."*

Joshua 1:8 also reminds us to meditate on God's Word to be prosperous and successful.

6. **Change your lifestyle and surroundings.**

    2 Corinthians 6:14 warns, *"Be ye not unequally yoked together with unbelievers: for what fellowship hath righteousness with unrighteousness? and what communion hath light with darkness?"*

7. **Seek professional help if needed.**

8. **Release it. Let it go and forget it.**

    Galatians 6:8 says, *"For he that soweth to his flesh shall of the flesh reap corruption; but he that soweth to the Spirit shall of the Spirit reap life everlasting."*

    Proverbs 22:24 advises, *"Make no friendship with an angry man; and with a furious man thou shalt not go."*

Walking in Purpose

Colossians 4:6 teaches, *"Let your speech be always with grace, seasoned with salt, that ye may know how ye ought to answer every man."*

What is holding you back from getting to your destination?

Don't let your past hurts affect your future. Ask yourself, *what's my purpose in life?* Pray, ask God to show you your purpose, and then live according to His Word. It's time to walk in your purpose.

I speak over your life right now that you shall live and not die!

Chapter Six:
Deliverance

We must pay attention to the warning signs and use them as a reminder to make the necessary corrections. There's a misconception that once you're saved and filled with the Holy Spirit, you no longer need deliverance. But that's not true. Spirits transfer, and they can still attack saved people. When going through deliverance, you must open up and tell it all to overcome the enemy. By confessing, you let the devil know that he no longer has authority over your life. Once that process is done and you are delivered, you will need to learn how to stay delivered. You will be able to recognize when those spirits try to attach themselves again. Stop holding on to those secrets. Release them, and I promise you'll feel so much better and lighter.

Walking in Purpose

Each of us must undergo deliverance to identify the underlying cause of the issue, discover a solution, and learn how to sustain our deliverance. Deliverance is an ongoing process. Occasionally, we think we're free from something, but we still experience triggers. That's when you need to evaluate and ask God to show you where the root still lies and seek deliverance once again. You can go through self-deliverance or work with people you trust—people who will honor your privacy and operate in delivery to help you get free.

In July, I was at a revival, and that's when God started really delivering me. On August 31, 2019, between 4:00 p.m. and 5:00 p.m. in Orlando, God completely delivered me from fear and everything else. That same year, at the end of December 2019, I was in a revival, and God completely delivered me from the pain of holding on to the

Walking in Purpose

trauma of being molested and sexually assaulted.

If those things were still attached to me, the old Dominique would have been running and screaming from the dog. The dog would have devoured my entire body. But I thank God for the wisdom and deliverance He has given me.

Don't let fear and your past stop you from what God has planned for you.

Chapter Seven:
Forgiveness

You need to get out of that toxic environment and enter into a healthy one. We know that being in toxic environments or relationships leads to mood swings, depression, suicide, guilt, and excuses. We often make excuses for others, try to justify their behavior, and find ourselves compromising on things that go against what we stand for. Sometimes, we lower our standards just to keep them in our lives out of the fear of being lonely. We keep them around, trying to fill that void.

You may ask, "Why is there a void in your life?" People in these situations often struggle with low self-esteem (low self-worth). Sometimes, things that happened in their childhood affect their lives and often lead to unforgiveness.

Walking in Purpose

To move forward and live a healthy lifestyle with peace of mind, forgiveness is key. However, granting forgiveness can be very difficult Once we extend forgiveness, it's crucial to let it go and move on and forget it.

Staying angry at someone only gives them control over your life. Forgiveness is crucial—for your own sake. Forgiving those who wronged you and truly letting it go will set you free. As long as you hold grudges, you are giving them permission to control your life, and you remain in bondage. Holding onto anger will damage you mentally, physically, emotionally, and spiritually. How do you expect your ministry to flourish if you're operating in manipulation and witchcraft and refusing to forgive?

Being manipulative, controlling, and abusing your authority as a leader is not of God—it's witchcraft. Take time to examine yourself and ask God for His plan for your life. Pray and ask God to cleanse you: Lord, forgive me. Purify my heart, and take out anything that's not like You. Lord, as I decrease, may You increase. We must kill the flesh daily.

What is the purpose of holding grudges?

Lyft Moment:

Everyone who knows me well knows that I had a fear of dogs. On Thursday, I picked up an elderly lady and dropped her off. She was a little weak, so I helped her with her luggage. As I went to drop her off, two little dogs tried to come out, but I managed to put them back inside the house. Then, as I was getting her luggage from the trunk, the pit bull suddenly came running toward me, sniffing me. I froze for a moment, and the dog stood there. I calmly told

Walking in Purpose

it to move, all while backing up at the same time. I got behind the older lady, and the dog started barking at her. I was praying, Lord, please don't let the dog bite us while I was still backing up. The lady started yelling, It's me, it's me, and the dog stopped barking. I jumped into the front seat and left the lady outside. The girl grabbed the dog, and I heard the owner yelling. Once the owner got the dog, I jumped out, grabbed the rest of the luggage, set it down, and quickly jumped back in my car, driving off. I was in shock from what I had just experienced.

They say dogs can sense fear, and I had been afraid of them for so long. Thank God I was delivered from the spirit of fear.

Chapter Eight:
Declarations

1. **I WILL walk in my calling and destiny. Lord, I will go where You want me to go, and I will say what You want me to say. Lord, order my steps.**

2. Go and walk in your anointing with confidence, head held high, and stay encouraged.

3. **Life and death lie in the power of the tongue! Keep your mouth off people!** When you sit and gossip about others, they will, in turn, gossip about you!

4. **The Word for Today is: Keep pushing toward your purpose.**

5. The labor pains are coming nonstop, but you have to be strong and endure the pain. When you are in delivery,

Walking in Purpose

birthing your purpose and destiny, it will all be worth it. **The world needs to hear you.**

When God reminds me of my assignment and purpose, He says, "Just do it, say it, and I will take care of the rest. Trust me, they are listening. Just let it marinate."

#GodITrustYou

6. I want to tell somebody, Don't **give up. You are going to make it.**

7. Be careful—**every door is not meant for you to walk through.** Be cautious, as some doors serve as traps, designed to divert your attention from achieving your intended destiny and purpose.

8. Don't worry about what people are saying about you. **Just do what God told you to do.**

9. It's time to embrace the call on your life. God removed them from your life for a reason. Just remember, **they**

Walking in Purpose

can't go where God is about to take you. So stop crying over spilled milk.

Made in United States
Orlando, FL
09 May 2025